Network, Navigate & Nurture:

The Equation to Strategic Networking

By Michelle Ngome

Line 25 Consulting, LLC

ISBN-13: 978-1500829506
ISBN-10: 1500829501
Published by Line 25 Consulting
First Paperback Edition

Author Photograph Kory Fontenot
Cover Design by San'Quan Prioleau

This book is available for special promotion, corporate training and bulk pricing. For details contact info@line25consulting.com.

DEDICATION

To my beloved mother and brother who have been a constant support through all my endeavors.

To the YPs Pursuing their Passions, the Power is within.

ACKNOWLEDGMENTS

I finally understand all the experiences in life have led me to putting these words on paper. The contributions for this book goes beyond the editor, designer and printing. I could list names, but the truth of the matter is every word of encouragement, speaking engagement and listening ear whether from a stranger or friend helped shape this book. Every contribution strengthens the platform that I stand on. I appreciate your support.

Table of Contents

Foreword

In late 2011, as my undergraduate college career was coming to a close, I began to consider the benefits of pursuing a MBA and other educational options with the solid intent of entering the work place. One significant suggestion from my peers that continued to recur was the absolute necessity of networking. One's work history, life experiences, and educational goals lead to a greater contribution at the academic level where teambuilding is strongly emphasized. I knew I was going to continue working full time, and I had an interest of being a full-time student. Beyond the university environment, I needed a way to supplement the networking aspect of graduate school.

Searching for other options, I looked into professional organizations that would complement my need to network. Similar to being a new student in the middle of the school year, it took some time and a deep breath for me to become acclimated to the new professional scene. Each time I stepped into an event, it was obvious that there were staunch relationships already formed, and I was hesitant to enter an ongoing conversation midstream. After leaving a social one evening, I made a promise to myself to meet at least one person each time I attended an event. Keeping to my promise, I saw progress immediately! Meeting one person, naturally lead to more introductions, and then, remarkably, I was "working the room" when I stepped out.

After a few months of scoping events and organizations, I became a member of the Houston Area Urban League Young Professionals (HAULYP) and the National Black MBA Association (NBMBAA) based on their core values of enriching the African American community through education, economics, and service. Remaining consistent and committed my new relationships lead me to job opportunities, business ventures, leadership roles, mentors and friends. That promise to myself has changed my world and has led me to writing *Network, Navigate & Nurture: The Equation to Strategic Networking*!

This book derives from a collection of my personal experiences and shared information from colleagues and friends. My concept is designed for those choosing to be proactive when meeting and greeting all prospective clients and provides the essential objectives to keep foremost in mind when attending events to more fully appreciate and enjoy the rewards of networking.

It is my hope that this book will encourage you to continue to enhance your business, professional and social skills. The value of nurturing relationships over time leads to mutual reciprocation. Every event, every encounter leads to a greater good.

Part One:
Networking Defined

"When you build trust, you strengthen your relationships, and get better results With, Through and For others."
— Dr. Randy Ross

I spent seven years in the financial services industry working with highly successful companies in a variety of roles. I never crossed over to investment banking, but I enjoyed reading the concepts of mergers and acquisitions, derivatives and commodities. In so doing, I believe networking is similar to the commodities market. According to *Investopedia*, a commodity is a basic good used in commerce that is interchangeable with other commodities of the same type. Is it a stretch; hear me out. When we network, we naturally surround ourselves with like-minded people. In most cases, we are putting ourselves on the market because we are looking for the missing piece in exchange to meet our needs at the time. What is our need? Could it be a career change, perhaps? Therefore, the missing piece would be an industry specific recruiter. With that as our main goal we venture out stating our employment needs to anyone who will listen. I use the commodities analogy loosely to explain that it takes at least two commodities to be in the market before they can be exchanged. Two resourceful individuals are required to become effective networkers. What value do we bring to the networking market?

1

Networking is one of the most essential skills needed to survive today. Regardless of industry, whether corporate America, entrepreneur or student, we need to know people to succeed in this world. In a professional environment, we may need a referral, a letter of recommendation, or a viable reference. If we are entrepreneurs, our networking may be the next lead to a client. One thing I have learned is not to take moments for granted. I like to say, "You never know who you are going to meet or where it may lead." As a professional, we must be ever aware of potential opportunities.

Networking is a supportive system of sharing information and services among individuals and groups having common interest. Networking is always tied to business; yet, our support system can stretch to hobbies, religion, and education. The important fact about networking is to remain professional at all times. We are all told to get out there and network. Where does one begin? Is it merely attending the next scheduled event with a few associates?

As stated earlier, many times when we begin networking, we are in search of a missing piece. If we are comfortable networkers we are building on our soapbox. We look to attend the best events and become acquainted with key people. Yet, we are hasty to get to the bottom line. True networking cannot be rushed. It is difficult to measure value in the arena of impulse. As it has been said time and time again, "…quality over quantity…"; we need patience to see quality unfold.

Let us refer back to the commodities example. There are several commodities on the market, and each one has its own influence. Hence, back to the question, "What value do we bring while networking? Not too long ago, while at an event, a businessman, and I exchanged introductions and he queried, "What can I do for you and your business?" I was unprepared for a response inasmuch as I had no business to offer. In retrospect, he had already provided the service I required, non-gratis. By his directness, his question and demeanor piqued my curiosity while providing a model for networking in action.

We must recognize our professional worth in such away that we can honestly, ask a professional question, and expect an honest answer to deliver a need on that requirement. I began to reevaluate my skills and my professional circle. When pursuing a raise or promotion, we believe we deserve a specific amount of pay because of our experience and quality of work. We contribute a portion of value to the company which should be reflected in our salary. Do we truly believe that our work exceeds our supervisor's expectations, or simply that we have been around so long we are due for a raise? Ouch! We can no longer attend networking events with the *"what's in it for me?"* attitude.

The first step in finding value while networking is embracing a level of authenticity. Shifting our mentality from self-seeking to being genuine, our energy changes and everything else falls into place. Our guard comes down as people get to know the real person. Early on, I would doubt myself because I felt I had the skills, and I was acquainted with a few key people within the company who could help me to transition into a management position at the bank, but always to no avail. I eventually eased off on my pursuit for a management position, and began expressing interest in other financial roles and companies without expectation. I wanted to know what else was available in banking besides the brick and mortar. Although not quite ready to leave other opportunities, I began to consider my options. I always scrolled the job board but never applied. One day my supervisor came up to me and suggested that I would be a good fit for an operations analyst position that was open. I reviewed the job for a second time, and within weeks I became an operations analyst, a pivotal role as the department was moving from Baton Rouge to Houston.

In Stephen Covey's <u>The 7 Habits of Highly Effective People</u>, he discusses how synergy is the highest activity in life by applying creative cooperation through our social interactions and relationships. Remaining authentic creates a natural synergy among those whom we encounter. Our service is in direct proportion to your networking. We become a resource when people can tap into our capabilities, creation, and problem solving skills. When people clearly recognize our skills they are able to place us where we seem fit. One may tell me what he can do, but once I see his work, those results become tangible to me. From there I can assist, collaborate, or refer him to another credible source. Let us become active networkers on the basis of authenticity and mutual reciprocation.

READY, SET, PITCH

Most people find it difficult to network while others are great conversationalist. Some are too timid and do not feel comfortable initiating a conversation; yet, others talk freely regardless of the person. You cannot separate networking from the elevator pitch.

So how does one begin his or her pitch? "Hi, my name is Michelle Ngome. I am the lead consultant with Line 25 Consulting, a marketing firm." That is not a bad introduction if I am trying to obtain a client. It is a typical introduction and it is what we have been taught throughout the years. We have all heard and practiced our thirty-second elevator pitch. How many of us like the elevator pitch? Some believe it comes across as a salesman and claim not to be a salesman. Yet everyday we are selling ourselves to someone for various reasons. Whether it is for employment, offering our products or service, or even advice. Our pitch is stating highly acceptable opinions of ourselves that we want others to believe making us the best person for the position. So, how do we customize this pitch to our specific liking?

We all know the saying, "It's not what you know, but who you know." While reading The Wealth Choice by Dr. Dennis Kimbro, he expands it by saying; "It's what you know about who you know as well as who knows you." There it is again. Everything leading to the word *value!* What value do we bring? Craft your elevator pitch in such a way that it shows the value we offer during the introduction. We have less than 60 seconds to capture someone's attention by providing the best description of ourselves. With society focused on *"what's in it for me?"* mentality; one has to be quick and engaging.

Hello, my name is Michelle Ngome. I manage Line 25 Consulting a digital marketing firm specializing in marketing strategy and public relations. We help clients align their marketing goals while increasing their visibility through digital platforms.

In those few seconds, I am able to inform my prospect about who I am and the business solutions my company offers to clients. If the person is interested that leaves room for open-ended questions to continue the conversation. For example, "What do you mean digital platforms?"

Our platforms may be as simple as building a client website, social media training, and public relations.

By asking an open-ended question it shows attentiveness and interest. Keep responses concise and effective to maintain the flow of the conversation. More importantly, interject an open-ended question to show interest towards an individual. There may or may not be a potential business match. With quality introductions, it allows us to consider future opportunities. I have been to several events where I have introduced people on the spot because they have expressed mutual interest. There is no need for me to be stingy with my contacts.

Please keep in mind it is possible to have more than one elevator pitch. If our clientele varies or we are in a career transition, make sure the foundation to the pitch is solid. Allow the elevator pitch to remain flexible. Hone in on and practice using these skills and with self-assurance that they can be applied to multiple industries while conversing. Being knowledgeable of how and when to use the pitch effectively is a basic necessity.

Several years ago, I attended a speed-networking event. Each table held a group of six people allowing each person 30 seconds to give his or her pitch. This one gentleman at my table was first to go, and needless to say he took the whole three minutes. He explained his degrees, certifications, experience, and business. Of course, it was impressive the first few seconds, but then it became down right inconsiderate. The other people at the table missed their opportunity to provide their pitch and exchange business cards. This guy is intelligent, but he was neither engaging nor considerate of people's time. Whether we are attending an event or in the elevator at work, our pitch should be keen and magnetic.

THE CONVERSATION

So much emphasis goes on the elevator pitch that we should not lose sense of our natural ability to have a conversation with anyone. One reason most people are overwhelmed by the thought of networking is the thought of walking into a room with several groups of people immersed in conversation. Hesitation kicks in and we are intimidated with thoughts of where we might fit in? How do we begin? Timidity can be minimized and overcome. I encourage scanning the room for a familiar face. The colleague we recognize serves as our precursor. Unknowingly this person allows us to warm up to the environment, the flow of conversation, and eases our anxiety.

My friends tease me because I prefer to attend event by myself. For me, when I go out by myself, it mentally prepares me to speak to someone. I cannot rely on my friend, and I do not have anyone depending on me all evening. It may seem minute, but our friends are our comfort zones, and sometimes we do not want to lose focus even if it is for a few minutes. To this day, I first acknowledge those that I know first before sparking conversations with others.

7

The key to starting a conversation is to show interest. It is that simple. I enjoy hearing about people's stories. In Alan Garner's Conversationally Speaking, he states how you can expand on that interest by three topics to get the conversation going:

- Consider the situation.
- Consider the other person.
- Consider yourself.

With three ways to begin:

- Ask a question.
- Voice an opinion.
- State a fact.

Before making an approach, I look for the following;

1. **Eye Contact** – When two people make eye contact it means that they acknowledge each other for that moment. If there is a short distance between the two, initiate the approach with a smile and an extended hand out to greet them. This typically allows the other person to put his guard down and for me to proceed with a friendly 'Hello.'

2. **Groups** – When approaching a group, be mindful of the interactions among the individuals. Step in, acknowledge everyone with eye contact, extend a handshake, then be attentive to the speaker. Two positive things can happen here; there will be an opening to express an interest with a question or statement, or the speaker will wrap up and turn the spotlight on the newcomer.

3. **Speaker** – I love meet and greets as they always turn out as motivational experiences. Do not be intimidated by the host

or speaker of the event; more than likely they are the reason you decided to attend the event. Seize the opportunity to interact with them. I have received autographed books, advice, and other treats just by taking the time to say "Thank you," to the speaker. I believe this is by far the easiest part of networking. When approaching a speaker, consider asking a question or stating a key identifier on his topic and how it resonated with a relevant interest. Use the speakers' platform as your gateway to approach him.

4. **Open Ended Questions** – Those of us who have worked in sales work in sales are very familiar with the reasoning behind open-ended question. These questions allow for fluid engagement between parties which allows one to obtain necessary information while building rapport in the process. When in doubt, keep in mind that *how* and *why* questions are great conversation starters. The following are some examples of both closed-ended questions and open-ended questions;

    Closed-Ended Questions
    Are you a member?
    Have you been here before?
    Are you looking for a job?

    Open-Ended Questions
    What are the benefits of becoming a member?
    How often do you attend these events?
    Which companies have you applied to so far?

My colleagues have observed me actively engaged in conversation to any and all attendees at a given event and are often curious about what I am talking about while networking. Open-ended questions start the conversation, but the topics will determine the flow of conversation. First, we know politics and religion are off limits, so, what topics can be discussed? I prefer to exchange business cards in the beginning and use that as a conversation piece if necessary. Glancing at an individual's card, allows me to populate questions based on a readily identifiable industry and career. Second, a good habit to form is to spend 15 minutes a day either watching or reading local and national news to stay abreast on current events. Topics to consider are community news, sports, upcoming events, projects, employment, industry trends, music, film, and my favorite lavishing compliments. Once again, it is about being authentic and expressing sincere interest. By paying a compliment reveals similar interest and likeability albeit within a given time restraint.

There is no definitive answer for how much time to allow when interacting with others. I have been in situations where a precious five minutes has been wasted; yet, a generous 45 minutes has resulted in a valuable addition to my treasure trove of contacts. Many variables are at play. As I mentioned before, the businessman asked me "What can I do for you and your business?" that conversation was less than three minutes. His question can be viewed as positive or negative depending on how one interprets the question. His directness was positive; his approach lacked tact and negatively came across as a numbers game i.e. questions 1, 2, 3, exchange cards, and repeat. Do not attempt to be that person whose primary objective is to touch base with everyone in the room.

In addition, if someone avoids eye contact, constantly checks the time, and gives only terse responses, it may be time to wrap up the conversation. Either enough time has passed or there was not enough substance to sustain the conversation. Such an incident is not to be taken personally as there can be several factors regarding the interaction. More importantly, end the conversation on a high note.

Novices often misjudge when the time has come to conclude the conversation. The real world is not a speed-networking event, and no bell will ring as a signal to move on to the next person. Encounters with small groups will prove to show some conversations in full sync while others are dull. Either way, it is important to handle the conversation gracefully. The best way to close with someone is by saying "It's been a pleasure speaking with you and good luck with everything." *Everything* is an acceptable substitute against recanting specific details from the conversation. If business cards were exchanged, offer a timely follow up with a phone call, email, or social media. There is no trick or fancy way to end a conversation, but the professional world expects it to be polite and forward.

BUSINESS CARDS

Are business cards still relevant in this day and age with the advent of social media and apps? Debate over this old-school standard as ensued I am pro business cards as I believe it is personable and an extension of my brand. So many of the business cards I have received in my hand conjure a memory of the person, the place and the conversation. Is the business card vital for networking? In my opinion, this is a non-negotiable issue. It provides a basis for conversation and is an immediate reference to potential relationships. Occasionally, there are those who do not have a business card. They are eager enough to provide their contact information; however, it is the card that serves as a visual reminder of who we met. Whether we are accepting contact information via phone or business card, jotting down notes serves as a good reference when the time is right to initiate contact. I also encourage students and job seekers to obtain business cards if they are actively networking and seeking career opportunities.

Information on your business card should include your name, email address, website or LinkedIn profile, business address, and phone number. As space provides, you may add your social media handles, logos or pictures, quotes, slogans, or taglines. Also, make sure your information is valid. I remember an encounter with a meeting planner and sharing a great conversation about a speaking opportunity for me at an upcoming event. The next day, I attempted to reconnect with her, but all was in vain. Not only was there no email address but also two invalid websites. Being persistent, I called and left a message but I never received a response. I regret the fact that a potential connection got away. Handy solution--cross out defunct information and replace it with a neatly written upgrade. People want to stay connected to you for a reason.

Entrepreneurs will want to align business cards with websites and other marketing collateral. With the exception of meeting someone, the website maybe the first evidence of your brand. In the absence of a website, all contact information should be accurate, current and referenced to an active LinkedIn profile.

Before entering an event, make certain the placement of your business cards and cell phone are accessible. Women who carry oversized handbags, take heed! Nothing creates a more inept image than seeing a female frantically rummaging through her purse and patting herself down for a cell phone or a business card while trying to continue a conversation interspersed with lame excuses. Trust me—I have been guilty of this and I have learned the hard way. Being able to readily hand over a business card allows for smooth continuity of a progressive conversation or a positive lead up to conclude a conversation with dignity.

With the popularity of smartphones there are a few apps that convert business cards to digital contacts. I am still operating in traditional methods; the up-on-it-user will find these apps helpful.

1. **SnapDat** (iPhone) – Information is stored as a traditional business card format and easy to exchange.
2. **CardMunch** (iPhone) – Powered by LinkedIn. scans the card and is saved to contacts and makes LinkedIn profile visible.
3. **CamCard** (Android & iPhone) – Similar to CardMunch, a scanned card is saved to phone contacts. It syncs the card across all its users' devices.

Networking *Defined* provides a comprehensive approach to recognizing our own value and being able to present it to others, which can be coworkers, associates and potential clients. Self-discovery allows us to be authentic in our approach when dealing with people from all walks of life. Our elevator pitch must capture our audience closely authenticate normal conversation. We are ready to navigate the networking maze.

Part Two:

Navigating The Professional Maze

The great city of Houston, by its sheer size, offers incredible diversity and a plethora of options for any professional. Anytime I want to try something new, I ask a friend or look online to see what is out there. When the networking bug came to me right before graduate school, I had no idea whom to ask. My friends and I fraternized, but we did not network. When I went online, I came across several events and organizations that were quite relevant. I started making my rounds at different events, but felt stagnant. The progress that I thought was going to come so easily was not there. It is naïve to assume that networking is simply about attending events and collecting business cards. To overcome this obstacle and come to understand the value of others, devised a complete networking plan which served as a guide me along this faltering path. I made the commitment to meet one person at each event and met my own goal all the while recognizing that the road was becoming smoother.

NETWORKING PLAN

According to the U.S. Bureau of Labor Statistics, 70% of all jobs are found through networking. As much as I socialize, such a high percentage was surprising to me. With such a high rate, it is important to have a networking plan in place if you are in search for that missing piece. First, I have a networking partner for accountability. Every week, we discuss upcoming events and the associated cost. Then we decide which event may be more important to attend. We operate on the basis of divide and conquer, and follow up by discussing contacts and potential leads. In addition, we share a networking calendar through Google Drive (calendar syncs to phone with alerts). Next, I created a networking plan. The plan does not have to be extensive; it can be one page outlining purpose, goals, interest, and notes. Take time each week to plan a schedule and review successes and failures about each event. This plan may change each month as progress and accomplishments are tracked. The plan serves as a guide with the following breakdown:

1. **Purpose** – Why am I networking? I am networking to expand my social circle for future career opportunities.

2. **Goals** – What do I want to accomplish while networking? I want to attend at least two events per week and become a member of a supportive organization within six months. I want to attend one conference each year.

3. **Interest** – What type of events am I targeting? My targets are young professionals (YPs), marketing, and finance organizations.

4. **Organizations** – What type of groups or organizations will be the best fit for me? I joined HAULYP and NBMBAA.

Keep in mind that this is a mock template to be critiqued to meet changing needs. Once I had my template, I could logically consider how to select events. With my networking plan, I went into overdrive. I became more structured with my schedule and found ways to gain immediate value from events. I felt in charge with the combination of finding valuable people at value-based events.

THE BUDGET OF NETWORKING

"There is nothing in saving money. The thing to do with it is to put it back into yourself, into your work, into the thing that is important, into whatever you are so much interested in that is more important than money." Henry Ford

Networking is an investment of time and money. We are visibly aware of the duration of an event, but do we ever consider the financial aspect of networking. The majority of events are free and often occur around happy hour. There are events that charge an admission fee and those fees will accumulate over time. Consider the additional costs of membership dues, seminars, conferences, coffee breaks and lunch meetings. Combine professional overhead expenses with monthly living expenses, early morning latte's, and entertainment with family and friends, and it becomes apparent that one must find a realistic solution one to become a financially sound networker.

When I decided to embark on my networking journey, I failed to consider the financial aspect of it at all. I dove in head first filling my calendar with enticing activities with a variety of groups. I naturally gravitated to free events, but quickly discovered that with every event there is always a beverage and sometimes a meal. Consider seeking out reputable organizations who allow non-members' fees versus becoming a full-fledged member. At some point, it becomes an extra expense with which to be reckoned. I eventually extended my budget to include networking events and incorporated that into my networking plan. I am not a financial genius, but I can provide a common-sense approach to meeting financial obligations. I recommend as follows:

1. **New or Increased Budget** – There are two options here. We must either allocate funds specifically for networking or decrease our entertainment (social) budget. This can be tricky depending on one's lifestyle. Most of us are familiar with shuffling things around to meet our desires accordingly.

2. **Envelope System** – This system allows for each category to have a designated dollar amount. Once that balance dwindles to zero, no further expenditures can be made until the envelope is refunded. I was able to adopt the envelope system only for networking. Each pay period I withdrew $50 specifically for networking events. It was important for me to have cash available. I believe when you have cash it makes you reconsider the value of events.

3. **Volunteer** – I suggest for major events such as galas and conferences volunteering. As conferences are held annually,

it allows one to be in a better position to prepare and save. Volunteering is a good way to save money and stay in the mix. More on this later.

I am frugal by nature, and it does not help that I have a financial background allowing the cost of networking to be foremost on my mind. Strongly consider the events or organizations to be attended and the associated costs which can include, a paid luncheon, a light evening, or conference registration. Networking is just one aspect of investing in ourselves. Put the dollar where the value is.

THE MAZE OF EVENTS

Every city is different with its options of events. I have compiled a list of options to start off in the right direction. Although it may sound familiar, I have been able to leverage these resources effectively. Hopefully these suggestions will provide you with a different perspective on your journey.

EVENTBRITE.COM

I may be the only person who goes through the Eventbrite listing on a regular basis in search of upcoming events. I am sure we are familiar with the site on a registration standpoint, but consider that other groups are hosting events as well. I have been informed about all types of events from seminars, conferences, as well as social events. What I like most about scanning through Eventbrite is that I can register for an event two months out, and it will automatically syncs to my calendar, and I will receive reminder emails close to the event.

MEETUP.COM

This is one of the quickest and best ways to get out there. Meetup.com is the world's largest network of local groups. It allows one to create a profile based on zip code and interest and it will filter a list of local groups. Each group shows the number of members, upcoming events, and discussions in order to gauge their activities. Meetup.com serves all individual from various backgrounds. By joining at least two active groups, one's social calendar will forever be filled.

AFFINITY GROUPS

This is really important from a professional standpoint for one looking to move up the corporate ladder. Some employers provide affinity groups, JOIN NOW! Why? This is one of the biggest steps towards upward mobility, and it is effective. I have been fortunate to work with J.P. Morgan Chase and Invesco Investment Services, and each has several groups to select from whether it caters to women, African-Americans, Latinos or Hispanics, GLBT, sports, event planning, and community service. The benefit of participating with an affinity group is the fact that one has the opportunity to meet people in other departments and learn about various job functions. Playing kickball with one's supervisor, coordinating an event with a department head, or serving food with the Chief Marketing Officer brings the VIP's within reach. All of this is possible when we attend company functions beyond working hours. It allows us to see colleagues in a different light whether it is their competitive edge in sports or their generous heart through community service.

Furthermore, by spending ample time with the company means we are a fully invested employee. I remember when I was in banking it was emphasized to me that the more accounts an individual has the less likely he or she is to switch banks. Banks start us off with a checking account linked to our direct deposit; before long, we have a savings account, credit cards, an auto loan, and a mortgage. Before we know it we have become so invested with your bank that it would be burdensome to move our accounts to another financial institution. It is the same with one's employer if we become fully engaged. If we participate in work activities or hold more important responsibilities we are less inclined to leave the company. The work-social component provides a fulfillment that exceeds your eight-hour shift.

One thing I realized by participating with these types of groups is the inner dynamics of the company. I am not referring to company gossip, but truly understanding the structure, key people, and what it takes to navigate through the corporate maze. I have had people advise me how to get in good graces with a specific manager, how to interview for the next position, and how to be self-sustaining in the corporate environment. One's participation with an affinity group is a good transition if we are applying for internal positions or have become a candidate for a promotion. Our colleagues are aware of your involvement with the company, which could easily become a topic of conversation during an interview. Consider the high school student example: Do colleges want the bookworm that is a straight-A student with no outside activities, or the well rounded A/B student with many extra curricular activities? Most people want to be surrounded by other the well-rounded people. It is desirable to balance work with pleasure in the workplace.

PROFESSIONAL ORGANIZATIONS

Overall, professional organizations have served the greatest benefit for my career. There are hundreds of organizations from which to choose, therefore, it is imperative to be strategic when making these choices. I encourage everyone to select a niche and a general-purpose organization. A specialty organization is important in order to remain current with industry trends. These types of groups broaden your knowledge through workshops, seminars, and conferences providing the latest industry information. Examples of specialty organizations are the American Marketing Association (AMA), Society for Human Resource Management, or Women's Energy Network to name a few. These highly concentrated organizations serve well for those seeking employment within a specific industry.

A general-purpose group attracts individuals with diverse backgrounds who choose to interact for common interest. This is especially important for business owners, as this provides a pool of potential clients for both business-to-business (B2B) and business-to-consumer (B2C). These organizations may include the Chamber of Commerce, Business Network International (BNI), or your local networking event. Religious affiliation, alumni associations, fraternities, sororities, and affinity groups also fall under this category.

For individuals between the age of 21-40 years old, there has been a rise of young professional (YP) organizations. These organizations may be independent or subsidiaries of more established parent associations looking to cater to their younger counterparts. YP's serve as a great starting point for those who are transitioning from college to the workforce and wanting to maintain the benefits of an organization while elevating their level of professional engagement.

In 2012, I made the decision to join the NBMBAA as my specialty organization. I was entering my MBA program that year. My second choice was the HAULYP, a service organization to serve my general purpose. To gain a better understanding of the organization's culture, I attended several events and spoke to members and leadership before committing. It is important to believe in the organization in order to meet our needs and become contributors towards the greater good of the organization.

CAREER FAIRS AND CONFERENCES

Career fairs and conferences may be the most overwhelming out of all the types of events. Size may vary depending on the program from a local, regional, or national level. These events contain several sponsors, vendors, speakers, and a host of other options for an attendee. It is imperative to understand why we are attending the event complemented with a plan of action.

When it comes to career fairs, research and preparation is key. Here are a few ways to maximize time at a career fair. Always go to the company site, view the current job openings, and apply beforehand. In doing so, one's cover letter should state that an intention to attend the upcoming fair. This gives you leverage as the recruiters may make preparation for an on-the-spot interview. If executed properly on each end, much time can be saved for both parties. On the other hand, we have all experienced waiting in line for thirty minutes to have a two-minute conversation with a recruiter stating, "Please apply online." If we have already made an online application, provide the recruiter a current resume, and allow him or her to take notes as the position is discussed in more detail. Get a business card, connect on LinkedIn, and make a timely follow up.

Several conferences hold large job fairs such as the National Society of Hispanic MBAs (NSHMBA) and the NBMBAA. These types of events may have hundreds of companies. In this case, select three to five strong companies. Take time to learn about each company and its involvement during conference. Several of the larger companies offer private receptions allowing for more intimate encounters with company leadership. During the 2013 NBMBAA Conference in Houston, one of my good friends attended a Coca-Cola reception where he cultivated good relationships with some of the top leaders within the organization. He was scheduled for an interview two weeks after the conference and the day after the interview, he was offered a position as a business development manager.

Conferences are the most expensive when it comes to networking events in light of registration, travel, lodging, meals, and entertainment. One way to minimize the cost is by volunteering. I strongly encourage becoming a conference volunteer if it is held locally. These organizations operate on the support of conference volunteers. In many cases, registering for a four-hour shift opens access to the entire conference for that specific day. Be mindful of the shift selection with regard to time frames. There will be specific workshops and speakers on the agenda. The 2014 National Conference on LGBT Equality Creating Change was held in Houston and my friend encouraged me to volunteer. I signed up for one four-hour shift. My first day had such a positive impact that I decided to sign up for extra shifts. I had a chance to hear opening remarks by Mayor Annise Parker and keynote speaker Laverne Cox from *Orange Is The New Black*. I partake in dynamic sessions with great panelists along with engaging a tremendous amount of networking with people from all over the U.S. Although volunteering serves as a part time job, one can find creative ways to benefit from the event as a whole and in so doing connect with as many people as possible. Networking at a conference can rapidly expand contacts and productivity.

With hundreds of quality conferences held each year, it can be difficult to decide which ones to attend. First, attending a conference is an investment of money and time. The significance of a conference is to discuss areas of interest, whether it is industry trends or social issues. Conferences serve as an educational opportunity to review the current state of affairs within a given industry and determine how the associated profession can be moved forward.

Virtual conferences are on the rise and will surely become more appealing over time. Consider virtual conferences as a series of *webinars*. Such conferences are relatively inexpensive. Registration tends to be cheaper and travel, lodging, and meals are not required. Similar to a live conference, multiple sessions are offered along with the benefits of being able to download material and recordings after the event. Krista Jackson, founder of Women CEO Project, holds The Women of Power Virtual Summit, a three-day conference comprised of speakers from a wide range of locations providing great insight on their industries. Topics included social media, finances, business structure, and strategy. What I liked best compared to my previous experience with virtual conferences is that the presenters were back to back. With fifteen speakers, I didn't have to select which sessions to attend. I was able to *attend* the event from the privacy of my home and while multi-tasking on other projects. If there were anything significant that I missed, I was able to retrieve the recordings in my spare time.

RELIGIOUS AFFILIATIONS

I suggest that religious affiliations be considered as not only a place of worship but also an opportunity beyond the spiritual experience. Religious institutions are becoming more holistic in their approach to their congregations. In lieu of or in addition to attending regularly scheduled services, one can benefit by participating in a ministry and a host of other activities. Joining a ministry allows to tapping in to one's skill sets and share information with other like-minded people. I have encountered those who remain on extreme ends when it comes to religious practices. That is to say they are either highly involved or only attend sporadically. Those who regularly attend worship services may have other agendas such as seeking career opportunities and business dealings among like-minded people.

I had a colleague hear me speak at the Houston Area Urban League's Small Business University on marketing strategies. Impressed with my presentation, he believed I would be a good fit to speak for the CEO Ministry at his church. I gladly accepted and spoke on Managing Facebook for Business. I embraced the intimate audience as everyone was either a business owner or poised to transition into the business world. That speaking engagement gave me a monumental opportunity to distribute all of my marketing collateral and meet influential people. More importantly, I was invited back to host a workshop! Religious affiliations do matter. Do not be constrained, but rather consider that a place of worship can be a community where one's resources can be maximized through membership.

COFFEE VERSUS LUNCH

Previously, I discussed a sensible approach to establishing a networking budget. One alternative to coffees and meals is *Google Hangout!* It is beyond doubt that coffee or lunch is an ideal one-on-one for exchanging cards. However, this venue can quickly become a costly proposition. One must be attentive and purposeful as to whom we spend our time with after an event. Meeting someone for coffee sets the tone as an affordable, quick, yet personable. Deciding to have lunch with someone suggests an intention to spend quality time with the expectation of discussing a variety of topics. In most cases, a coffee break will last 15-30 minutes, whereas lunch will be a minimum of one hour at best.

Regardless of the occasion, these are straight-forward questions to consider. What is the purpose of our meeting and what do we hope to gain? Are we hoping to establish rapport, gain insight into a company, advance on a career opportunity or give a more detailed client pitch? Any post networking encounter should have well-defined objectives in mind with a better-than-average expectation for positive results. The precursor is to have prior insight. Be knowledgeable of the potential contact with regard to his or her company profile and standing. Be prepared with a mental list of questions to address at the meeting. At the very least, visit his or her LinkedIn page before the engagement.

Navigating through events and keeping up with acquaintances is no easy task. However, if we mindfully set goals, take action, and remain resourceful we can maximize resources and reduce expenditures. With so many options, networking too can become costly, but we must consider it as one of the most invaluable resources to use as professionals. Embrace it.

Part Three:

Navigating In The Digital Space

"We don't have a choice on whether we Do social media, the question is how well we Do it."

—*Erik Qualman*

How many of us have tried *Googling* ourselves? Become keenly aware of what is available for the public to view including photographs. With that being said, how likely is it that our offline connections will inevitably become online. There is a real possibility that we will eventually connect with our online followers. What image have we presented to our followers?

I initially was going to title the section *Navigating from Offline to Online*, as there seems to be a missing piece with taking connections from offline to online. A few items to keep in mind social media serves as an efficient manner to follow up and maintain communication with contacts. Second, over time allow your online connections to translate to direct contacts and eventually a lead. Third, maintain dependable and viable contacts. Lastly, with so many platforms available, we must make sure we remain personable while consistently contributing valuable content to our followers. Each platform has different levels of engagement depending on how we utilize information to our benefit. Social media has changed the way we communicate so we must look into the avenues that enhance our online presence.

WEBSITES

First, given the resources and skills to build a personal domain is a tremendous asset. Whether we are an employee or an entrepreneur, our personal website can become the initial phase of having an online presence. If we choose to write a sports blog, an online resume, or present a portfolio, we are at liberty to do so. Our website provides us with creative control and leads us into the realm of being a subject matter expert. A website should reflect information that is important to our career and our position in that career would be wholesome to share with society. One's personal website can transform over time depending on the current need. My website www.michellengome.com has been a music blog, my grad school vlog, and now my public speaking page. When doing a Google search with my name, my website ranks third and includes images from my site. If we choose a over-used name, we will have to become more creative with a domain name. More importantly, becoming an influence obtaining a personal domain is an asset.

SOCIAL MEDIA STATISTICS

Employers and businesses rely upon the use of social media. According to *U.S. News Money* clearly explains how hiring managers apply social media during the recruiting process:

- 92% use LinkedIn to gain an overview of professional experience, tenure and skills.

- 24% use Facebook.
- 14% use Twitter.
- 94% use social networks during the recruiting process.
- 93% are likely to look at candidates' social media profiles.

In terms of social media within the business realm, *Business 2 Community* provides us with the following:

- 97% of all consumers search for local businesses online.
- 78% of small businesses attract new customers through social media.
- 87% of businesses view social media as a highly successful element of their marketing mix.
- 60% of all social media referred traffic to a business website coming from Facebook, Twitter and/or LinkedIn.

LINKEDIN

LinkedIn is known as the most professional platform among all social media networks. Make sure the posted profile is a 100% complete; add keywords, along with a professional headshot. Anytime I obtain a business card I ask the individual if they are current with LinkedIn, and I connect with them within three days by adding a personal message. LinkedIn establishes immediate credibility. A profile consists education, work experience, skill sets, and interest. Employers or clients are able to view a profile to consider a possible candidate. Another way to complement an online presence is by requesting recommendations and placing that on a personal and/or company website along with marketing material.

Gaining a high profile on LinkedIn requires that all information is concise, current, and relevant to the objective. Articles on business, professionalism, education, and leadership are abundant. It is best to post in the mornings by 11 a.m. Select a favorite topic and become well versed by producing consistent content. Search for your industry specific groups that will be of most benefit in given industries, target markets, alumni groups, and local groups. Provide feedback and encourage discussions in any group that allows a forum for entering personal expertise in a given field that will stand out in the discussion. Remain knowledgeable on industry trends and be available to share that information with others both online and offline.

The power of LinkedIn lies in the second connections to expand a network. Any member's profile is readily available showing connections through mutual relationships, skill, interests and location. Connections are easily made by requesting a mutual contact for an introduction to a third party of interest. While surfing the net, I came across an article on new R&B artist for 2014. I was so excited by this article and I felt like the writer and I had similar tastes in music, and I was sure she would like my client. I cross-referenced the journalist on LinkedIn and noticed she had attended college with one of my colleagues. I sent an email to my friend asking for an introduction. A mere two contacts and a few days of patience resulted in an email form the journalist. I emailed the music link immediately, and we began to share correspondence.

Do not rush the time it takes to build a relationship. Often, we are so anxious to get to the decision maker and stop short before reaching him or her. The decision maker is all important, but we must not overlook the gatekeepers. In most cases, we consider the gatekeeper to be the receptionist at a corporate office. Let us consider, also, the analyst, the junior marketer, or in this case the journalist. The writer provided me with valuable information on how my client could grow and attract attention through the publication. The information that the gatekeeper provides prepares us for the time when we speak to the person in charge. Another perspective, what if the journalist starts her own publication? I have established a good rapport that will carry on regardless of career moves. Let us establish credibility early and nurture lasting relationship.

GOOGLE PLUS

If Google is your friend, then Google Plus is your best friend! Many would agree that Google knows everything. How many of us can live without a Google product? Google Plus is the only social media platform that has a direct impact on search engine optimization (SEO) with any post. If offering business advice or promoting oneself, this is a major plus.

What makes Google Plus the upper echelon in social media? Having 1.1 billion users is just scratching the surface. It is the efficiency of the additives such as Circles, Communities, and Hangouts. Although other platforms have similar features, Google seems to be far more efficient. Circles allows us to group people we know including family, friends, coworkers, or the option to create a group. Therefore, when we post we have the option for our post to become visible to a specific group or to the public. Communities allows us to select an industry or topic and become a part of the discussion. In each community there are professionals that provide valuable content to the group. Lastly, the item that I love the most is Google Hangouts. Similar to Skype, it is a great alternative if we are not able to meet someone because of distance or time constraints. Hangouts can carry up to ten people with shared screen access. I have conducted interviews, consultations, and meetings on Hangouts. Depending on your purpose for the Hangout, the whole event can be uploaded to YouTube. If you have a Gmail account, the company has made everything quite efficient with its platform and continues to redefine technology. (*Please keep in mind that YouTube falls under the Google platform and the combination of the two enhances online presence tremendously.*)

FACEBOOK

In my opinion, I used to consider Facebook to be the most intimate of social media platforms. I have had to reconsider since more people search my name before they consider my company page. The whole of my business content is on my business page, but I do include some business content on my personal page. Social media experts suggest that for every three personal post one business related post should also appear on a personal page. This is a great method to ease networking into personal expertise. Facebook has grown by incorporating groups similar to LinkedIn. It also has affordable ad rates to promote business pages or personal posts.

TWITTER

Twitter may be the most efficient and quickest way to meet someone online. Twitters' 140 character interactions makes it easy for individuals to access the minds of CEO's, celebrities, and trendsetters. People are able to share information instantly. I have been very successful on utilizing Twitter to gain media contacts. Participating in Twitter chats allows one the opportunity to increase followers and gain insight from industry professionals. It is good practice to follow influencers, share their tweets, and then contact them directly in an appropriate matter. Make sure your tweets and retweets are interesting and informative.

INSTAGRAM AND PINTEREST

I was really hesitant to enter either of these platforms. However, both are great from a branding standpoint. This is the time to showcase a logo, images, and more importantly, let people know we are active networkers. People become more engaged with pictures and videos. Make the most of photo captions and hashtags to increase engagement. As we continue to be a visual driven society these two outlets are perfect venues for personal branding efforts.

SOCIAL MEDIA MANAGEMENT

We maybe thinking, "I am just one person. How will I manage these five networks?" It can be a bit overwhelming at times. Anytime I do social media training, I advise new individuals to pick one platform to master and then gradually learn the other platforms. It took me years to become active on Twitter and even longer to join Instagram and Pinterest. I began to use these platforms once I recognized the value for each one based on my transition going from exclusively personal to applying it as a business tool. If we are comfortable with Facebook, we can begin dropping our branding jewels on our personal pages before transitioning to a business page or another network.

Moreover, if we already have accounts with each platform and are looking to remain active and efficient, there are several tools that allow us to do so. These management tools allow us to add multiple platforms, schedule your posts, and have them released in an uniformed manner. HootSuite is my personal favorite as it allows up to five free social media profiles before applying a monthly fee. Buffer, TweetDeck, and SproutSocial are other popular managing tools. If we use one of these tools, allow the content to remain relevant to the appropriate platform. Just because you can type one post and send it to all doe not mean you should. Keep in mind there may be friends on multiple platforms, and they will see that same message at the same time on each network. In addition, be timely with real time posts. Do not appear lackadaisical on any social media efforts. Social media allows us to become creative with our marketing efforts and the management tools enable our productivity.

EMAIL SIGNATURES

It is not uncommon to send and receive 100 emails a day. We all know how to compose an email; email signatures remain underused, but may be an essential piece to your branding. It can serve as both a marketing tool and a reminder to people in regards to your association. An email signature should be brief consisting simply of your name, company, position and contact information. Additional social media handles may be optional. Here is an example of my current email signature:

Michelle Ngome
Management | Marketing | Public Relations
Line 25 Consulting
713.xxx.xxxx
Instagram/Twitter: Line 25 Consult
Facebook: Line 25 Consulting

An email signature serves as a virtual business card. I email a multitude of people and businesses that I have a very slim chance of meeting. Upon receiving my email and viewing my signature, they have a description of me, and access to my cyber world. If we want to become really creative, we might consider using Wise Stamp, which allows us to create a very unique signature with our social media handles.

EMAIL OR PHONE CALL

Whether to email or phone call depends on the conversation we had during our face-to-face meeting. It is easy to send an email. If we are cordially following up, an email is best. One thing I consider is that if I have requested a connection on LinkedIn, I will send a message through that platform alone. However, if we believe that we have a better than average chance of connecting with someone who might lead us to our objective, we then take the more aggressive approach and make a call. I like to call someone within two days of meeting him or her with a real hope that our recent conversation is still fresh on his or her mind. A phone call is direct and more personal.

Whether offline to online, it is imperative to sustain credibility among our peers. Just as we practice proper etiquette and uphold common courtesies in direct contact we can translate that to enhancing our online and offline presence. Provide followers with valuable content on a consistent basis. Find the platform that works the best, and exercise it to the fullest capacity.

Part Four:

Nurture The Leaders

*"Leaders must be close enough to relate to others,
but far enough ahead to motivate them."*
— *John C. Maxwell*

It is important to define our goals in life whether they are personal, educational or career motivated. I know in a fast paced society it is hard to carve out extra time for additional responsibilities such as community service. Taking time to give back to the community helps improve schools and support families. In addition, it aids in personal and professional development. As a volunteer one becomes part of a team surrounded by people of diverse backgrounds that can lead to positive relationships and future opportunities.

VOLUNTEERING

I whole-heartedly believe in giving back to the community, and along the way, I have made firm contacts and friendships in doing so. Volunteering allow us to congregate with individuals who have the heart to serve. Prior to my involvement with organizations, I would volunteer on occasion with nonprofits. Each nonprofit is different with its process, and it can become a bit cumbersome. I realized it was easier for me to reach my community service goals through my involvement with professional organizations rather than on an individual basis. Several organizations, churches, and affinity groups engage in activities that give back to the community whether it is back to school drive, food drive, or helping out at the food bank. We all value our time, but we must find a way to serve our community on a regular basis. It may be the most rewarding work you do as an adult.

Volunteering with the right organizations connects us with advocates as we broaden our knowledge on social issues. Learning from community members provides a good balance as we navigate between the two environments of corporate and community. As a volunteer one lends their talents, discover interest or leverage corporate resources to raise the public awareness on community issues. I have been fortunate to obtain advice from corporate personnel, local government administrators or seasoned entrepreneurs. I was able to meet with these people on the basis of shared interest through edifying the community by our service.

MENTOR

Just as people say, *"Networking is key for success,"* finding a mentor is the ascendancy towards that path. Selecting a mentor wisely can vastly impact your life. It may be a short process that happens naturally, or it can be a strategically long process. Just as you have friends for different purposes you may have more than one mentor serving different purposes. A mentor can be pivotal to your education, professional development, and lead to surpassing possibilities.

I remember my first mentor was at the age of thirteen. My

family dynamic had shifted and I was approaching my first year in Atlanta. I was fortunate to join a summer program called Post Secondary Readiness Enrichment Program (P.R.E.P.). At the time, my life was chaotic; my emotions were unraveling, and a young lady by the name of Samandra Demons became my first mentor. Her energy and sound wisdom steered me in the right direction. For the first time, I had a promoter behind me. Her influence enabled me to embrace all the changes I was going through at the time. The program showed me the upside to college. My mentor instilled an unsettling drive that has remained with me until this day.

Realize that the people we encounter plant seeds in our lives. It may be words of encouragement and wisdom at any given time. How do we nourish the seed? Samandra planted the seed of ambition. No matter the numerous change of majors in college or career changes, I always had a plan with a timeline that I was willing to execute to the best of my ability. I encourage all to find a mentor as soon as a shift in your life becomes evident whether it is education or career. Take time to review the networks scroll through your social media sites, and make a list of people who are intelligent and influential. From there, consider elevating a relationship with those people and contact them as quickly as possible.

Consider the search for a mentor as an application process; look for the best candidate to meet your immediate needs. Draft a list of questions and characteristics that are important to you to determine which person is the best fit. Some mentor qualities to consider are:

1. **Personality and Intelligence** - Consider positive interpersonal relationships. These are the people we spend

time with in and out of the work environment. This is important, as everything is not always centered on career decisions. It may be the initial intention, but it will naturally progress into one's personal life. Observe how people adapt to environments and other personalities in the room. Is this person friendly? Do they practice common courtesies such as offering introductions you to people or extending invitations to events? Also consider his or her business acumen and if it will be an asset.

2. **Work-Life Balance** – As we progress in our education, career, or entrepreneurship our lives become more demanding. We most desire the leadership of someone who can relate and advise us at all times. This is where questions of experience will come into play; how did we move up the corporate ladder? How did we manage the transition from corporate to entrepreneurship? Why should we pursue a M.B.A. or other professional certifications? If we hold a professional job, we must find a mentor in our industry and ideally in our company who can guide our steps as we grow.

3. **Network** – In seeking a mentor, the ideal is to target someone who is not only influential but who also has influential network. A mentors' network should be significant, as he or she will ideally bridge the gap to our objectives minimizing the gamut of engaging an introduction. A true mentor will be willing to share opportunities. He or she will be forthcoming to offer relevant information in a given industry and will be able to suggest key people.

For a second time, I was fortunate to find a mentor through natural progression. While I was holding a board position with the NBMBAA, Darrell James and I would constantly exchange ideas about the organization. Soon, he became influential enough to further my business ideas, my transition to entrepreneurship, along with the creation of this book. Holding a board position gave me a platform among the community that allowed me to interact with many people. Under Darrell's leadership, I encountered more personable and sincere introductions and was exposed to other opportunities that I would not have known about otherwise.

MENTEE

Once a mentor has become established, the real work is just getting started. "No matter where you are in your journey, there's always someone you can help show the way," Keith Wyche. Communication is going to allow for a good mentor-mentee relationship. Just as we are interviewing for good a mentor, there are questions we should ask ourselves. In this current moment of our life, why do we need a mentor? Where do we want to be in the next three to five years, and who can help us get there at a realistic pace? We know ourselves better than anyone, but here are some qualities to enhance the relationship with a mentor.

1. **Cordial and Aggressive** – An oxymoron at its best, traits are necessary in business. The reason why I state to be cordial and aggressive is that we need to let our intentions be known while we are networking. State the needs, and get the points across quickly. We are all busy. There is no need

to waste precious time or offer excuses for our self or our mentor. A mentor should be accountable for appointments, advice, and connections. Do not hesitate to send reminders or follow ups.

2. **Focused and Consistent** – When working with a mentor, we must be hyper focused on individual goals. Ultimately, we are the ones who will be held accountable. Meetings with a mentor should serve as a progress report. What have we accomplished in a specific timeframe? Allow your updates to be consistent with each meeting? Do not become actively stagnant with several extant ideas with no means to execute. Arrange priorities and work until the goal is reached.

3. **Open and Available** – Just as we need to be cordial and aggressive towards the things that we want, we need to be receptive to offers. We will receive an abundance of advice, instructions and challenges from our mentor. Be receptive, and adhere to sound wisdom. As we mentally open to advice, we must also be physically available for opportunities. If our mentor is available to extend his or her network to us through emails, conference calls, meetings, and events it is important that we comply with those opportunities.

The characteristics mentioned above allow you to search within yourself and consider your true desires as you progress towards your path of personal professional development. As I used myself as an example earlier, when I found a mentor I had to step up to the plate. I am definitely one that becomes hyper-focused on goals, but my mentor allows me to narrow my focus, directs me to what matters the most, and holds me accountable.

Although I do not consider myself a mentor, I make sure I remain active with ties to the community. I make efforts to speak to students of all ages about my education and career journey through organizations such as The Organization of Black Aerospace Professionals (OBAP), local schools, and universities. Fourteen years ago, when I was a high school senior, a gentleman spoke my class about college and passed out a blue card titled "Success Principles". I have no recollection of what he said, but I still have that card as a constant reminder of what it is I have to do. By reaching my goals I am reaching my community, and hopefully, my efforts can impact a student much as that long-ago speaker's principles have resonated with me.

The mentor-mentee relationship thrives on the basis of reciprocation. Yes, the mentor is an authority figure; yet, the mentee is still in position to teach. Knowledge is shared information that from which all may benefit when communicated. As the mentee role results in accomplishing goals, in return the mentee becomes the mentor. Always remember that someone helped direct our path throughout life.

Closing Thoughts

Although I displayed networking in four parts, the truth of the matter is we are always simultaneously performing these actions. We are continuously nurturing relationships which is how friendships are born from which initiatives spring forth. Genuinely connecting with someone allows us to naturally develop a relationship. Someone trusts that we are the best person to hold this information, the best person for this role. We have become the best person over time because of the effort we have put forth.

Networking is a lifestyle. It is self-marketing at its core. It is not something to do when business is slow or if we are seeking a job. Allow networking to be incorporated on a regular basis, just as if we were going to the gym, engaging in hobbies, or studying for an exam. Be strategic. Be proactive. Remain valuable. Devise a plan that makes one step out of our comfort zone when it comes to our approach to networking. Explore organizations in different communities, cultures, and demographics to broaden your awareness. We always extend our personal brand with our best foot forward and let service be a part of those steps. Whether it is extending your skills or connecting two people together.

Radiate confidence while navigating. The way we navigate your network may present our next big opportunity. T.D. Jakes states in his book <u>Instinct</u>, " A net only works if it's thrown. A Network only works if it's utilized." Our relationships are our best resources. Leverage every opportunity so that we may *Network to your Net worth*!

Last Words

I am sure whatever your path is in life you will succeed. Continue to invest in yourself through people, books and the numerous resources available to us all. I thank those that have invested their time and money in this book. I hope my experiences and practical knowledge helps you grow in your networking journey and beyond. Continue to invest in yourself and nurture relationships.

If this book met or exceeded your expectations please consider the following:

- Write a review on Amazon, Google Books, iBooks.
- Post about this book on your blog or social media: Facebook, Instagram, Google +, Twitter and Pinterest.
- Recommend this book to friends, colleagues, co-workers, students, bloggers, sales associates, introverts and extroverts the possibilities are endless.

Please stay in touch. Share your questions and stories with me, as I will make every effort to respond.

Contact Info:
@Line25Consult (Twitter & Instagram)
www.michellengome.com
emailme@michellengome.com

If you would like to me to attend an event or other professional inquiries please email me at info@michellengome.com.

References

Covey, Stephen R. *The 7 Habits of Highly Effective People: Powerful Lessons in*
Personal Change. Free Press, 2004

Garner, Alan. *Conversationally Speaking.* McGraw Hill, 1997

Jakes, T.D. *Instinct: The Power To Unleash Your Inborn Drive.* FaithWords, 2014

Kimbro, Dennis. *The Wealth Choice: Success Secrets of Black Millionaires.* Palgrave Macmillan, 2013

WEBSITES
www.bls.gov
http://www.business2community.com/social-media/103-compelling-social-media-marketing-statistics-2013-2014-0679246#!bb0JEN
http://money.usnews.com/money/blogs/outside-voices-careers/2013/09/11/want-to-get-a-job-fast-become-a-social-media-savant

About The Author

Founder of Line 25 Consulting and Line 25 Entertainment, specializes in management, marketing, and public relations for multiple industries. Michelle has garnered over ten years of experience in marketing and finance from corporate settings, nonprofits, and small to medium business enterprises. Past clients include Houston Area Urban League, Twice Media Productions, Lone Star College, Texas Southern University, Windsor Village CEO Ministry to name a few.

Michelle is actively involved in several professional organizations such as the Houston Area Urban League Young Professionals (HAULYP), Houston Black Leadership Institute (HBLI), National Black MBA Association (NBMBAA), The Recording Academy, and Women In PR. She has had the opportunity to serve in leadership roles for HAULYP and NBMBAA.

Michelle graduated with a B.B.A. in Finance from University of Houston Victoria and has a M.S. in Internet Marketing from Full Sail University.

For more information please visit the following sites:
www.networknavigageandnurture.com
www.michellengome.com
www.line25consulting.com
www.line25ent.com

49